SOME EFFECTS OF GENDER ON THE MEANING OF "WORK"

SOME EFFECTS OF GENDER ON THE MEANING OF "WORK":

AN EMPIRICAL EXAMINATION

by

Elizabeth A. Martin, Jennifer Hess, and Paul M. Siegel[1]

Bureau of the Census

Introduction

This paper is concerned with fundamental questions about the meaning of

the term "work": namely, what qualities of activities warrant their description as

work, and which sociocultural and situational factors influence lay interpretations

of activities as work? The original motivation for asking these questions was

primarily methodological. It arose in the course of a program of research

conducted between 1986 and 1993 to redesign the Current Population Survey, the

national labor force survey which is the source of official U. S. estimates of rates of

unemployment, labor force participation, and other labor market measurements.[2]

The CPS instrument does not define technical meanings of key concepts (such as "work," "job," "business," and "looking for work") for respondents, but instead

relies upon their intuitive understandings of these terms. It was suspected that

respondents held varying interpretations of labor market concepts, and that these

differences might result in misreporting of certain activities or for certain

subgroups in the population. For example, the National Commission on

Employment and Unemployment Statistics (1979) suggested that teenage

employment was probably underreported in the CPS by the older respondents who

typically give proxy reports for teenagers. Underreporting bias can occur because

teenagers engage in marginal employment, and the older respondents who report

for them have different (and perhaps too restrictive) interpretations of the types of

work activities which should be reported in the survey.

In order to investigate sources of bias and ambiguity in labor force

measurements, the Census Bureau and Bureau of Labor Statistics (BLS) undertook

a series of investigations to explore the frames of reference and common

definitions for key survey concepts held by the public, and to identify other sources

of response variance in labor force measurements. The main purpose of those

investigations was to identify problems in the questionnaire which could be

corrected by rewording, clarifying, or reordering questions, adding new questions,

revising response categories, improving training for interviewers, etc.

Questionnaire revisions were tested in a series of split-sample experiments,

eventually culminating in a redesigned automated questionnaire which was

implemented in July 1992 and becomes the official source of labor force estimates

in January 1994 (see Polivka and Rothgeb, 1993). Although the sole purpose of

our research investigations was to improve labor force measurements in the Current

Population Survey, the results also provide substantive insights into the varieties

of interpretations of the meaning of work in U. S. society, and some of the

sociocultural factors which influence those interpretations. In particular, in this

paper we consider the influence of gender upon the meaning of work.

We begin by considering the official definition of "work" in the Current

Population Survey, and we review some previous results from the cognitive

investigations of its meaning conducted as part of the CPS redesign. Next, we

present an analysis of data from an experiment designed to identify gender

influences on interpretations of work, and we discuss the implications of our

findings.

The Measurement of Work in the Current Population Survey

The Current Population Survey counts as employed all persons who were

"working" during the week containing the 12th of each month. "Work" is not defined, per se, but "employment" includes only work for pay or profit, which encompasses salaries and wages, piece rates, commissions, tips, or payment in kind. In addition, work for the purpose of earning a profit or fees on a family business or farm is included, whether or not an individual actually had any earnings. Volunteer work, school work, and housework are explicitly excluded from the official definition of employment.

This definition is of broader interest than as an arcane matter for methodological research. "Work" as defined in the CPS represents the official identification of the activities regarded as economically productive in the U.S. economy. Over the life of the Current Population Survey, the official concept of work has changed little, although from time to time there has been controversy about the exclusion of certain activities, such as housework and childcare, from the official definition of work.

Debates about the official definition may be grounded in broader disagreements about the meaning of work. One way to explore such conceptual issues is by use of hypothetical vignettes. Vignettes have been fruitfully used in sociological research to investigate variations across the population in social definitions and normative judgments, such as what constitutes sexual harassment or child abuse, the fairness of earnings and the severity of crimes (see Rossi and Nock,

1983; Wolfgang et al., 1985). Here, we analyze respondents' classifications of

vignettes describing hypothetical work-related situations. The vignettes were

administered as part of a debriefing interview conducted with respondents

immediately after they had completed a regular CPS interview conducted from the

Census Bureau's computer assisted telephone interviewing (CATI) facility. All of

the vignettes described classification situations thought to be marginal or

ambiguous from the point of view of respondents, such as setting up or working in

a family business or working for a few hours (which should be reported as work),

or volunteer work (which should not be). Respondents were instructed, "I asked

you a question about WORKING last week. Now, I'm going to read a list of

examples. After each example, please tell me whether or not you think the person

should be reported as WORKING last week," then were given examples such as,

"Sam spent 2 hours last week painting a friend's house and was given 20 dollars.

Do you think he should be reported as WORKING last week?" In the first such

vignette study, conducted in 1988, Campanelli, Martin, and Creighton (1989)

found that respondents held very diverse interpretations of work, and that only 8

percent of respondents gave answers to all 5 vignettes which agreed with the CPS

definition. The most common response pattern was too inclusive, and the next

most frequent response pattern was far too restrictive, excluding all marginal work activities, even those which CPS counts as work. Moreover, respondents'

interpretations of work varied systematically with age, with younger respondents

interpreting work more broadly, and older respondents holding narrower, stricter

interpretations. The correlation of age with interpretations of work lent support to

concerns about possible underreporting of youth employment by older proxies.

A second respondent debriefing study was conducted in 1991. Its primary

purpose was to compare the revised and the old CPS questionnaire, in a split-

sample CATI survey in which each household, selected by random digit dialling,

was randomly assigned one of the 2 instruments. As part of this study, a

respondent debriefing interview (including vignettes) was again administered by

CATI immediately following the regular interview, to test whether the

questionnaire revision had improved respondents' comprehension of key concepts

and phrases as intended. The respondent debriefing interview incorporated an

additional feature intended to identify possible gender bias in classification of

activities as work. The gender of the person described in the vignette was

randomly assigned by varying the name (for example, in the vignette above, a

random half of respondents were asked about "Sam" and the rest about "Diane").

We hoped to learn whether respondents were influenced by gender in interpreting

activities as "work." The vignettes represent only a limited number of dimensions on which activities which might be regarded as work could be arrayed. Thus, while the data in hand can show interactions between gender and some properties of activities that affect their perception as work, we do not claim to have represented the full range of such properties.

Evidence from diverse sources certainly supports the possibility of gender bias in what sorts of activities are regarded as work. For much of the 20th century, large segments of the U. S. population, both male and female, have objected to a married woman working, if she had a husband to support her (Duncan and Duncan, 1978). (Approval of a married woman working rose from about 20 percent in 1945 to 71 percent in 1971.) Duncan and Duncan (1978) further find that large majorities of the Detroit population believed that there were some kinds of work women should not have. This view had declined from the 1950s, but was still held by 62 percent of women and 74 percent of men in Detroit in 1971. Normative judgments which hold that women should not engage in certain kinds of work, or perhaps should not work at all, may well be based on different conceptions of what activities are properly "men's work" or "women's work." While interest in the distinction between "men's" and "women's" work has usually centered around the properties which confer gender on work, that is, what makes a set of activities men's or women's work, our interest here focuses on the identification of situations in which gender interacts with characteristics of activity in bestowing the status "work". A particular interest might be in whether a man doing "women's work" is regarded as "working".

Evidence from the CPS itself suggests that women's work activities are underreported, relative to men's. Probing questions asked to identify work activities which were unreported in the regular CPS interview showed that 1.68 percent of men compared to 5.40 percent of women had worked for at least a few hours but failed to report it (Martin and Polivka, 1992). This gender reporting bias may be due to the fact that women are more likely to engage in the kinds of employment which tend to be underreported no matter who does them. Alternatively (or additionally), respondents' reporting of work activities may be influenced by gender.

Three sorts of gender influences are possible. First, male and female respondents may have generally different interpretations of what should be reported as "work." Thus the same activities may be reported differently depending on the respondent's gender. We began with no specific hypotheses about overall male-female differences in interpretations of work. Second, a respondent's judgment of whether a person's activities should be reported as work may be influenced by that person's gender. Thus, the same activities may be reported differently depending on whether a man or woman is doing them. We hypothesized that marginal work activities were less likely to be interpreted as work when women were doing them than when men were. This hypothesis is consistent with the underreporting of female work activities. Third, there may be an interaction between gender of respondent and gender of the person he or she is reporting about. We hypothesized that male respondents would be more influenced by the gender of the person they were reporting about than female respondents would be.

Analysis

For each vignette, we examined the cross classification of response by gender of respondent by gender of the subject of the vignette. Table 1 reports results for each of 7 work vignettes which were included in the debriefing interview in the 1991 survey. Because the wording of the revised question about work in the new version of the questionnaire was designed to influence interpretations of the vignette situations, results are reported only for the old questionnaire version[3]. Prior methodological research shows that interpretations of "work" are less constrained in the old questionnaire than in the new. Thus, Martin and Polivka (1992) find that under the old questionnaire, respondents invoke a wide variety of criteria and judgments when asked to explain why they classified the vignettes as

they did. In contrast, the new questionnaire focusses respondents more exclusively

on the criteria of pay or profit. In consequence, respondents are less likely to

classify as work, activities which do not appear to involve pay or profit, and more

likely to classify as work those that do. Given the present paper's interest in gender

differences in meanings of "work", the difference between the old and revised

questionnaires is a diversion, since it introduces considerations of the differences in

meanings or understandings of "pay" and "profit". Instead of examining the

contrast between questionnaire versions, we focus on the old version because it

provides an opportunity to learn about gender biases in a context in which the

interpretations of "work" are relatively unconstrained. Of course, in our

questionnaire design and methodological work, we hoped to eliminate any potential

gender bias in reporting of work activities in the CPS.

TABLE 1 ABOUT HERE

Loglinear hierarchical models were fitted to each cross classification

(computations were performed using SAS) in order to evaluate the effects of

subject gender, and respondent gender, on the odds of a "yes" versus "no" response

to each vignette. The goodness of fit of each model is evaluated using the

likelihood ratio x^2 value obtained by comparing observed frequencies with the frequencies expected under the model. Models associated with probability less

than .05 fit the data poorly and must be rejected; we tend to regard models

associated with probability between .05 and .10 as marginal; models associated

with high p-values provide a good fit to the data. Specific effects (or sets of

effects) (such as the effect of respondent gender on vignette response or the

additive effects of respondent and subject gender on vignette response) may be

tested by comparing the chi-square values of alternative models which are

comparable except one includes and the other excludes the effect (or effects)in

question. A significant difference indicates the effect contributes significantly to

the fit of the model. (The use of the difference chi-square to compare and select

loglinear models for multi-way cross classifications is explained by Goodman,

1971, and is the procedure used here to select a best-fitting model for each

vignette.)

In the loglinear analyses of these 3-way tables, the first hypothesis

mentioned above -- respondent gender affects whether a particular activity is

thought of as work -- corresponds to a "main effect" of respondent gender on

vignette response. The second hypothesis -- respondents' judgments of a particular

activity are influenced by subject's gender -- corresponds to a "main effect" of

subject gender on vignette response. The third hypothesis corresponds to a three-way interaction involving respondent gender, subject gender, and vignette response.

In addition, after categorizing the vignettes as work or not, the respondents were asked why they had classified them as they did. That is, respondents who said that a particular vignette described work were asked, "Why would you consider that person to be working?" and respondents who said that it was not work were asked, "Why would you not consider that person to be working?" Following an initial review of the verbatim responses, categories were developed for similar types of answers and each verbatim response was coded to a category in order to quantify the responses. These materials will be employed to gain more insight into the ways respondents thought about the properties of activities which qualify them as work.

Results

In the following discussion, the seven vignettes are arranged into three groups: activities in which there is direct cash payment, business activities, and helping activities. These attributes were more or less deliberately built into the vignettes to ensure that they represented problematic situations from the point ov view of respondent interpretations. That these vignettes describe ambiguous activities, is clear in Table 1, where it can be seen that only for vignettes 6 and 7 does agreement among respondents exceed 80%. About 87% of all respondents said vignette 6 does not describe work and 89% of all respondents thought vignette 7 did qualify as "work". (In both cases, the consensus opinion is consistent with the CPS definition.)

Direct cash payments

Vignettes #1 and #4 describe a common type of marginal employment which has long been suspected to be underreported in the CPS: casual labor, or work for a few hours involving direct cash payment. In both situations, substantial minorities of respondents, about 20 percent for vignette #1 and 40 percent for vignette #4, report that the situation should not be reported as work (although it is covered according to CPS rules).

As can be readily seen in Table 1, neither respondent gender nor the gender of the subject of the vignette influences classifications of vignette #1. Fitting loglinear models to the 3-way classification of response, respondent gender, and subject gender confirmed the absence of gender differences in vignette 1: the best-fitting model is the model of independence ($x^2=1.37$, df=3, p< .72).

Table 2 shows that the model of independence also provides an acceptable fit to vignette 4. However, for this vignette, a model which includes the effect of respondent gender provides an even better fit. (The improvement in fit is marginally significant statistically, as shown by the $x^2 = 2.82$ ($= 3.18 - .36$) with df $= 1$ ($= 3 - 2$) which is associated with a probability less than .10.) The best fitting model includes an effect of respondent gender on the classification of the vignette, while the effect of subject gender is not strong enough to be seen in these data. This model significantly reduces x^2 relative to the independence model, giving us some justification for trusting the evidence of our eyes from Table 1 that men are more likely than women to treat this casual activity as "work".

TABLE 2 ABOUT HERE

The effect parameter for respondent gender does not tell us what aspects of this vignette are being differentially fastened upon by male and female respondents -- we see the vignette offering duration (2 hours), the activity itself (painting), the fact that the act was performed for a friend, and that compensation ($20) was involved. Analysis of the verbatim responses to questioning about each respondent's classification of the vignette shows that 43% of those who did not think the vignette described work referred to friend or friendship. Only 1.7% of those who thought it did describe work made similar reference.

Business activities

The second group of vignettes has to do with business-related activities. These vignettes test the notion of 'work for pay or profit' (see the official definition, above) since each vignette explicitly denies that the subject received any compensation for the activity during the week.

The best fitting model for vignette 5, cleaning up a back room in preparation for setting up a business, is shown in Table 3. The results indicate that the effect of respondent gender is significant. The positive effect parameter indicates that male respondents are more likely to classify the vignette as working than are female respondents.

TABLE 3 ABOUT HERE

In explaining their classification of vignette 5, male respondents are more likely than females to remark that the person in the vignette is "preparing to open a business" (42 percent male respondents [N=106] versus 30 percent of female respondents [N=167]). Female respondents were more likely to observe that "the business hadn't started yet" (17 percent of female respondents versus 9 percent of male respondents). Thus, in this instance, males appear to be more likely than females to understand this activity involving the possibility of future payment or profit as work.

We have already remarked in Table 1 that most respondents agree that a real estate agent who shows houses is working, even if they write no contracts.

The middle panel of Table 3 shows that in the ratings of vignette 7, neither

respondent gender nor subject gender have statistically significant effects. (The

best-fitting model is the model of independence: $x^2 = 1.78$, df = 3, p < .62.)

Vignette 3 describes unpaid work in a family business. Several different

models are fit to the data on this vignette in the bottom panel of Table 3. Model I,

which includes both the main effects, is rejected, with $x^2 = 8.34$ and p <.004 on 1

degree of freedom. Rejection of this model implies that a higher order three-way

interaction is needed to fit these data. Model II is the saturated model, which with

0 degrees of freedom necessarily must fit the data perfectly. The parameter

estimates for Model II indicate that, on average, respondent gender has a negligible

effect on classifications. However, respondent gender interacts with the gender of

the subject of the vignette. As can be seen in Table 1, men are highly sensitive to

subject gender, with 64 percent classifying "Amy's" activities as work, compared to

only 28 percent who classified "Joe" as working. In contrast, almost half of female

respondents classified the activity as work, regardless of whether a man or woman

was described as doing it. For men, but not for women, a husband who does

unpaid work in his wife's business is far less likely to be classified as working than a

wife who does unpaid work in her husband's business.

Verbatim responses indicate that, for male respondents, the absence of pay tends to be more salient when the subject of the vignette is also male. In response to the probe, 55 percent of male respondents who received the male vignette mentioned the fact that "he was not paid" compared to 42 percent of those who received the female vignette. Although the difference is not significant, it appears that men's classifications may take different factors into account, depending on the gender of the character in the vignette. The results suggest that a wife working without pay in her husband's business was more often perceived by male respondents as having a "real" job compared to a husband working without pay in his wife's business. The striking aspect of the pattern of responses shown for this vignette in Table 1 is that male respondents are more likely to describe it as work for a woman and less likely to describe it as work for a man than are female respondents, who do not appear to differentiate their treatment by the gender of the subject of the vignette.

Helping activities

The final group of vignettes includes activities in which the subject is helping out someone else without pay for the services. "Helping" activities include volunteering at a hospital (vignette 2) and babysitting one's grandson (vignette 6). While "helping" might be seen as feminine activity, it is not clear a priori that it is women's work. In fact, one might interpret the analysis of vignette 4 as indicating

that helping a friend is not seen as work, especially by women respondents.

Results in Table 1 indicate that, while most respondents do not classify

babysitting a grandchild as "work," male respondents are more likely to do so for a

female subject than a male. Female respondents are about equally likely to classify

the vignette situation as working regardless of the gender of the subject. Thus,

male respondents again appear more sensitive to subject gender than do females.

TABLE 4 ABOUT HERE

When Model I, which includes the main effects of subject gender and

respondent gender, is fit to this vignette in Table 4, the effect of subject gender is

significant but respondent gender is not. On the other hand, the p-value for the

model chi-square indicates that this model provides only a marginal fit to the data,

with $x^2 = 3.11$ on 1 degree of freedom and p <.08. Model II, the saturated model,

includes both of the main effects plus an interaction term. The interaction term is

marginally significant, with p <.10. Again, as seen in Table 1, the interaction term

reflects the fact that male respondents' classifications are polarized by the effects of

subject gender, with 23 percent of the men classifying "Ethel" as working

compared to 5 percent who so classify "Fred." This model shows the complex

relationship between vignette gender, respondent gender, and classification as work. Males are much more sensitive to the gender of the person whose activities they are judging than women are.

The other "helping" vignette (#2) shows an apparently similar pattern of responses. In this case, however, neither main nor interaction effects are statistically significant and the model of independence adequately describes the data (x^2 = 3.84, d.f. = 3, p <.28). Estimating the unnecessary interaction, Model II, for this vignette in Table 4 shows the effect parameters to be less than half the magnitude of the corresponding parameters in Model II for vignette 6. (However, a chi-square test indicated that the effect of subject gender was statistically significant for male respondents.)

Results reported above show that male respondents interpret helping activities differently depending on the gender of the helper, but female respondents appear unaffected by gender considerations. Examination of the verbatim responses suggests that male respondents apply the dimension of "payment" differently to men and women in these vignettes. In the verbatim responses for the hospital volunteer vignette, male respondents were more likely to mention the fact that the subject did not get paid if the subject was a male (64 percent) than if she was female (37 percent). About half of female respondents mentioned payment, both when the subject was a man and when the subject was a woman. These results are similar to those for vignette 3.

Discussion

Previous sections have detailed various gender differences in the classification of activities as work. While the treatment grouped the vignettes according to a typology of activity, our findings seem much more clear if we abandon that grouping, and proceed according to the nature of the effects we have found. That is, we fall back upon the discussion of main and interaction effects. In our discussion we limit our generalization to the rather artificial situation represented by the interview to respondents asked whether the person described in a vignette should be reported as "working last week, not counting work around the house." The fact that these classifications were collected after a series of questions about labor market activities must be kept in mind. We think these data tell us about how people define "work", but we cannot overlook the context of the evidence. It must also be born in mind that the universe of CPS household respondents offers a biased representation of the adult population.

First, there are two vignettes which show clear main effects of respondent gender, and in which there is no evidence of interaction between respondent and subject gender. These models have a clear interpretation as providing evidence of differences between men's and women's interpretations of whether a particular activity is work, regardless of the gender of the subject of the vignette. In our analysis of vignette 4 we found that female respondents are less likely than male respondents to interpret 2 hours of painting for a friend as work. The verbatim responses suggested that there was something special about friendship that causes female respondents not to treat it as work. The analysis of other vignettes makes it difficult to attribute this effect to helping. In our analysis of vignette 5 we found that male respondents were more likely than female respondents to classify preparations to set up an antique business in one's home as work, regardless of the gender of the subject. The verbatim materials suggested a gender difference in willingness to treat preparation for a business or investment in a future business, as work. For the situations described in vignettes 4 and 5, female respondents had somewhat narrower interpretations of "work" than male respondents.

Second, there are no vignettes which show correspondingly simple main effects of subject gender. That is, we have found no instances in which both male and female respondents agree in being more likely to treat an activity as work if it is performed by subjects of one than the other gender.

Third, subject gender effects are found, but only in models of these vignettes in which female raters are almost imperceptibly more likely to classify an activity as work if it is performed by a woman, and male respondents are more likely to classify the activity as work if it is performed by a woman. That is, models must include an interaction term--subject gender by respondent gender--in order for the subject gender effect to emerge. Despite appearances, only in the first of the two vignettes involving helping activities--uncompensated babysitting for a grandchild and unpaid volunteer service in a hospital--does the model require an interaction term indicating that helping by women is seen by men as warranting the description "work." In the final vignette helping is confounded with economic relations within marriage. Among female respondents, one spouse doing the accounting for the other spouse's business has about a 50/50 chance of being classified as work. Male respondents make a clear and powerful distinction on the basis of gender: they are much less likely than female respondents to classify a husband doing the accounting for his wife's business as doing work, and much more likely than female respondents to classify a wife doing the accounting for her husband's business as working.

Evidence from the verbatim responses suggests that male respondents apply the criterion of "payment" more stringently to men than to women when deciding whether the classify the person as working or not. For male respondents, "not being paid" was a much more salient feature in the vignette describing volunteer work in a hospital when the character in the vignette was male than when she was female. The evidence suggests that, for men, payment may be a more essential aspect of men's work than of women's work.

The analysis suggests that gender differences in the meaning of work arise out of the fundamentally social nature of work. People performing work have social relations with others around them, and we have found evidence that men's and women's interpretations of the same activity perfomed by men and women differs: "Helping" is "women's work", if you ask men.

REFERENCES

Campanelli, Pamela C., Elizabeth A. Martin, and Kathleen P. Creighton. 1989. "Respondents' understanding of labor force concepts: Insights from debriefing studies." Proceedings of the Fifth Annual Research Conference: 361-374. Washington DC: Bureau of the Census.

Duncan, Beverly and Otis Dudley Duncan. 1978. Sex Typing and Social Roles: A Research Report. New York: Academic Press.

Goodman, Leo A. 1971. "The analysis of multidimensional contingency tables: Stepwise procedures and direct estimation methods for building models for multiple classifications." Technometrics 13:33-62.

Martin, Elizabeth and Anne E. Polivka. 1992. "The effect of questionnaire redesign on conceptual problems in the Current Population Survey." Proceedings of the American Statistical Association, Survey Research Methods Section: 655-660.

National Commission on Employment and Unemployment Statistics. 1979. Counting the Labor Force. Washington DC: GPO.

Polivka, Anne E. and Jennifer M. Rothgeb. 1993. "Overhauling the Current Population Survey: Redesigning the questionnaire." Monthly Labor Review 116(9):10-28.

Rossi, Peter H. and S. L. Nock. (Eds.) 1983. Measuring Social Judgements: The

Factorial Survey Approach. Beverly Hills, CA: Sage Publications.

Wolfgang, Marvin E., Robert M. Figlio, Paul E. Tracy, and Simon I. Singer. 1985.

The National Survey of Crime Severity, NCJ-96017. Department of Justice,

Bureau of Justice Statistics. Washington, DC: GPO.

NOTES

1. This paper reports the results of research undertaken by Census Bureau staff. The views expressed are attributable to the authors and do not necessarily reflect those of the Census Bureau.

2. The Current Population Survey is conducted by the Census Bureau using a national multi-stage probability sample of about 60,000 households per year. Households are interviewed monthly for 4 months, then 8 months later are interviewed monthly for an additional 4 months. Household respondents report for all household members who are age 15 or older.

3. In the old CPS questionnaire, the determination that a person was working was based on a respondent's answers to the questions,

- "What was (NAME) doing most of LAST WEEK: (working, keeping house, going to school) or something else?" and (if respondent did not report "working"):

- "Did (NAME) do any work at all LAST WEEK, not counting work around the house?"

Interviewers were instructed to ask about unpaid work if there was a farm or business operator in the household, although there were no explicit questions in the questionnaire to make these determinations.

In the revised questionnaire, all respondents were asked "LAST WEEK, did ... do ANY work for (either) pay (or profit)?" (The reference to profit was included if the respondent had reported a business or farm in the household.) These revisions were intended to improve reporting of business activities, and to more explicitly communicate the concept of work for pay or profit.

www.ingramcontent.com/pod-product-compliance
Lightning Source LLC
Chambersburg PA
CBHW052028280526
45793CB00005B/1162